Intersections:
Where Faith and Life Meet

A Cumberland Presbyterian
Adult Resource
Volume 7, Faith

Discipleship Ministry Team
Ministry Council
Cumberland Presbyterian Church

8207 Traditional Place
Cordova, Tennessee 38016

First Edition 2015

Published by The Discipleship Ministry Team
General Assembly Ministry Council of the Cumberland Presbyterian Church
Cordova, Tennessee

ISBN-13: 978-0692482940
ISBN-10: 0692482946

We want to hear from you.
Please send your comments about this curriculum to
the Discipleship Ministry Team at chm@cumberland.org.

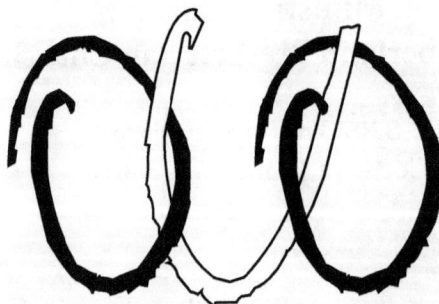

OUR UNITED OUTREACH
Made Possible In Part By Your Tithe To Our United Outreach

Table of Contents

Lesson 1   Sibling Rivalry 4

Lesson 2   The Man Who Would Be King...12

Lesson 3   Give Peace a Chance..21

Lesson 4   Lending a Helping Hand..30

Lesson 5   Virtue and Vice 39

Lesson 6   Peace Sayings of Christ 47

Editor: Cindy Martin
Designer: Joanna Wilkinson
Proofreader: Mark Taylor

To order, call 901-276-4572, x 252 or e-mail resources@cumberland.org.

Sibling Rivalry

Scripture for lesson:
Genesis 27:1-10, 35-38, 41;
32:3-5; 33:1-4, 10-11

I was an only child until my father and stepmother married when I was ten. Courtney, my stepsister, was about a year old at that time. Five years later, my half-sister, Calie, was born. The age difference was enough that I didn't fight all that much with either of my sisters, but were there ever some major fights between the two of them! As in almost every home where multiple children are raised, many of the arguments between my sisters occurred because one of them would get something (a toy, new clothes, extra privileges, etc.) that seemed unfair to the other one. It made for lots of yelling, screaming, crying, and not so many quiet, peaceful nights around the house.

Prep for the Journey

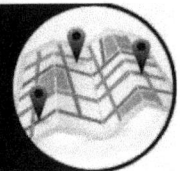

Jacob and Esau's story is straight out of a soap opera. Their mother, Rebekah, thought she was barren. But when she did finally become pregnant, the twin boys fought even in her womb. Esau was born with Jacob literally at his heels. Esau had all the advantages of being firstborn: the birthright, the lion's share of everything his father owned, and the promise of being the head of the household when his father, Isaac, died. However, he didn't seem to care about any of it. One day, Esau returned from a hunting trip, tired and hungry. He was so hungry, in fact, that he gladly sold his birthright to Jacob for a bowl of stew!

Because Jacob was Rebekah's favorite, she wanted him to have everything that was supposed to belong to Esau. God had already told her that Jacob was going to be the leader and that Esau would follow him. However, she decided to take matters into her own hands and make sure the blessing went to Jacob.

When have others placed a higher value on something belonging to you than you did? How did their opinions influence your thinking?

When and how have you experienced favoritism? What difficulties does favoritism create? How can it be corrected?

On the Road

Read Genesis 27:5-10.

Now Rebekah was listening when Isaac spoke to his son Esau. So when Esau went to the field to hunt for game and bring it, ⁶ Rebekah said to her son Jacob, "I heard your father say to your brother Esau, ⁷ 'Bring me game, and prepare for me savory food to eat, that I may bless you before the Lord before I die.' ⁸ Now therefore, my son, obey my word as I command you. ⁹ Go to the flock, and get me two choice kids, so that I may prepare from them savory food for your father, such as he likes; ¹⁰ and you shall take it to your father to eat, so that he may bless you before he dies."

At this point, the only hope Esau had left of receiving any of what had been his was to get Isaac's blessing. However, unbeknown to him, his own mother and brother were conspiring to get the blessing for Jacob. They planned to take everything by fooling Isaac into believing Jacob was really Esau.

Esau was at home, among his family. Our homes are supposed to be places of refuge. In a perfect world, home is where we go when the rest of the world doesn't accept us. It is where we go to find peace and receive comfort. We should be able to trust family members more than anyone else. They are supposed to be supportive and loving. So, when a family member betrays our trust, it is doubly difficult to understand, much less accept or forgive.

How can a person recover from that kind of betrayal? Yet there have probably been more times than we care to admit that we have been the betrayer, as well as the betrayed. We live in a world that lives by the rule, "Do unto others before they do unto you." It's difficult to accept that we likely cause as much pain and confusion as we experience.

> When have you been the victim of deception? How difficult was it to forgive the person(s) responsible for the deception?

> How can/do you respond to the attitude of "Do unto others before they do unto you"? What does your response say about your faith journey? What's the message behind this statement?

Scenic Route

Read Genesis 27:35-38, 41.

But he [Isaac] said, "Your brother came deceitfully, and he has taken away your blessing." ³⁶Esau said, "Is he not rightly named Jacob? For he has supplanted me these two times. He took away my birthright; and look, now he has taken away my blessing." Then he said, "Have you not reserved a blessing for me?" ³⁷ Isaac answered Esau, "I have already made him your lord, and I have given him all his brothers as servants,

Do you think Esau had the right to be angry with Jacob? Why or why not? Considering that Esau continued to live with his parents, how do you think he responded to his mother?

When have you entered a contract or binding agreement and later had regrets? How did you respond? What happened?

What does your name mean? Why did your parents give you that name?

Has an argument ever caused you or someone you know not to talk to a family member or friend for years? How did the estrangement affect others? What might have resolved the situation?

and with grain and wine I have sustained him. What then can I do for you, my son?" [38] *Esau said to his father, "Have you only one blessing, father? Bless me, me also, father!" And Esau lifted up his voice and wept....*

[41] *Now Esau hated Jacob because of the blessing with which his father had blessed him, and Esau said to himself, "The days of mourning for my father are approaching; then I will kill my brother Jacob."*

We can feel the anguish as it dawned on Esau exactly what had happened. Everything he had believed to be his, everything that legally should have been his, had been given to his brother.

Today many people want to know why Isaac didn't just take the blessing away from Jacob and give it to Esau. In this situation, modern understanding clashes with ancient tradition. The blessing that Isaac gave to Jacob was an irrevocable contract, legally binding. So when Isaac blessed Jacob, he gave away something he couldn't take back, which is why he waited until he thought he was on his deathbed before giving the blessing.

Today we often overlook the meaning of names. In ancient times, a name carried an important meaning. It is interesting to note that Esau said, "Isn't he rightly named Jacob?" The name *Jacob* means "to deceive." In order to understand many Bible stories and biblical characters, it is essential that we know the meaning of their names.

Even today, it is astounding how much the name of a person, church, or place can tell us. Names passed down through the generations tell us that family and tradition are important to that family. The name of a church can show what is important to its members.

Workers Ahead — CAUTION

Esau was so angry after Jacob cheated him out of his birthright and stole his inheritance that he vowed to kill his brother as soon as Isaac died. Jacob fled to the homeland of his mother and lived with her brother, Laban, for many years. While there, he married both of Laban's daughters, Leah and Rachel. God was with Jacob and blessed him with many children and large herds of animals. Yet there was still one thing Jacob lacked: peace with his brother.

Read Genesis 32:3-5.

Jacob sent messengers before him to his brother Esau in the land of Seir, the country of Edom, [4] *instructing them, "Thus you shall say to my lord Esau: Thus says your servant Jacob, 'I have lived with Laban as an alien, and stayed until now;* [5] *and I have oxen, donkeys, flocks, male and female slaves; and I have sent to tell my lord, in order that I may find favor in your sight.'"*

The two brothers were about to meet for the first time in many, many years. Jacob didn't know what to expect. He was terrified that Esau was still holding a grudge. He wasn't sure if Esau still wished him dead. So Jacob sent messengers bearing gifts to test the waters with Esau.

Read Genesis 33:1-4, 10-11.

Now Jacob looked up and saw Esau coming, and four hundred men with him. So he divided the children among Leah and Rachel and the two maids. ² He put the maids with their children in front, then Leah with her children, and Rachel and Joseph last of all. ³ He himself went on ahead of them, bowing himself to the ground seven times, until he came near his brother.

⁴ But Esau ran to meet him, and embraced him, and fell on his neck and kissed him, and they wept…. ¹⁰Jacob said, "No, please; if I find favor with you, then accept my present from my hand; for truly to see your face is like seeing the face of God—since you have received me with such favor. ¹¹ Please accept my gift that is brought to you, because God has dealt graciously with me, and because I have everything I want." So he urged him, and he took it.

Jacob took every precaution when approaching Esau, especially since Esau was coming with so many men. When they finally met face-to-face, Esau forgave Jacob, likening their reunion to seeing the face of God. After so many years, the weight of their broken relationship was lifted. The turmoil that had dominated so much of Jacob's life was gone.

There is no worse feeling than knowing we have wronged someone we love and respect. And there is no better feeling than being forgiven, especially when you know you don't deserve it. In order to live in community with other people, we must pay attention to our interactions and apologize when we wrong someone.

In the Rear View

It's a cliché that time heals all wounds, but it's a cliché for a reason. Growing older, gaining perspective, and getting the chance to correct our mistakes is part of our faith journey. Real relationships take work. True forgiveness takes effort. Peace, both in our world and in our lives, doesn't happen by chance. We can't just sit around hoping for things to get better; we have to do the legwork.

When have you felt the need to take precautions due to a broken relationship? What were they? How were they helpful or harmful?

What things happened when you were younger that you have felt guilty about? When has someone forgiven you for one of those things? How did you feel?

Travel Log

Day 1:

It is so difficult to find yourself at odds with your family. Think of a time when you have fought with someone you are very close to. If the relationship is still strained, contact that person and apologize for your role in the argument. Make some notes here of things you want to say.

Day 2:

The stress of the pain that we have caused others can weigh heavily on us. Often it is harder for us to forgive ourselves than it is to forgive others. Write a letter to God that expresses your feelings of guilt and despair over the pain you have caused. Ask for God's forgiveness. If you have not already asked for forgiveness from the person you wronged, do so now. Any time negative thoughts about this situation enter your mind, remind yourself that God has forgiven you, so you should forgive yourself.

Day 3:

Make a list of three people you admire for their ability to bring peace during difficult situations. Write a short paragraph explaining how they are able to bring peace.

Day 4:

Draw a picture of what it means to you to be forgiven when you know you've wronged someone you love.

Day 5:

It can be easy to withdraw into ourselves when a loved one hurts us. It's easy to pretend that words don't bother us. Sometimes people hurt us without even knowing it. Write down words that have hurt you in the past. Make note of why they hurt and how you can keep those words from affecting you in the future.

Day 6:

Take ten minutes out of your day to thank God for those people in your life who love you enough to forgive you. Write their names and a word or two about them in the space below.

Day 7:
   Create an acrostic using the word *PEACE*. (Hint: Think of a word that begins with each of the letters in peace.) The words should relate to peace.

P

E

A

C

E

The Man Who Would Be King

Scripture for lesson:
1 Samuel 15:35*b*–16:1, 13; 16:21-22; 18:28-29; 24:1-5, 8-22

A friend of mine, John, recently was fired from what he thought was his dream job. The money wasn't great, the hours were long, and the job was stressful, but John felt it was his calling in life. He recognized that he'd made some mistakes at work, but he couldn't believe those mistakes were enough to justify his firing. John recognizes now that the job was exactly what God was calling him to do, but the situation was not where he was called to be. It took a great deal of time for John to understand that a calling can change.

Prep for the Journey

God was the leader of the people of Israel. Granted, God had human representatives such as Moses, Joshua, and a series of judges, but they were basically God's spokespersons. When Samuel, the last of the judges, became old, the people asked for a king. They wanted to be like the neighboring countries whose kings led them into battle against their enemies. Even though God told Samuel to warn them what it would be like to have a king, the people insisted. God gave the people their wish and told Samuel whom he was to anoint.

Saul was the first king of Israel. At first glance, Saul was everything the Israelites could have wanted in a leader. He looked the part: he was tall and impressive. He had a commanding presence. He was very brave and heroic: he led the defeat of the Ammonites. He was very generous. Unfortunately, the reality of Saul was far less impressive than the aura he projected. His abilities and character didn't match the expectations people had of him.

Even though God had chosen Saul, he disobeyed God on many occasions. In fact, he failed to carry out God's command regarding the spoils of war in the first battle he led. He also set up a monument to himself, turning his back on God. It was not long until God regretted having made Saul king.

When have you fallen short of someone's expectations? How did it feel "not to measure up"?

Read 1 Samuel 15:35b–16:1, 13.

Samuel grieved over Saul. And the LORD was sorry that he had made Saul king over Israel.

16:1 The LORD said to Samuel, "How long will you grieve over Saul? I have rejected him from being king over Israel. Fill your horn with oil and set out; I will send you to Jesse the Bethlehemite, for I have provided for myself a king among his sons."

…13 Then Samuel took the horn of oil, and anointed him in the presence of his brothers; and the spirit of the LORD came mightily upon David from that day forward.

On the Road

Most people know at least parts of the story of David. He was brave, heroic, and "a man after God's own heart." He also sinned and experienced struggles. But this story begins shortly after Samuel anointed David, a young shepherd boy, to be the next king of Israel.

Read 1 Samuel 16:21-22.

And David came to Saul, and entered his service. Saul loved him greatly, and he became his armor-bearer. 22 Saul sent to Jesse, saying, "Let David remain in my service, for he has found favor in my sight."

Saul was often tormented by an evil spirit, and music seemed to calm him. Some of his servants knew that David played the lyre and also possessed many other good qualities, so they recommended that Saul seek out the boy. The relationship between Saul and David was very good in the beginning; Saul eventually made David his armor-bearer.

An armor-bearer was responsible for looking after, carrying, and repairing the king's armor. He made sure the armor was in good working order. Failure to do his job would have put the king in mortal danger. Because the king was often a primary target during battle, the armor-bearer had to be unafraid of danger. Obviously Saul thought David was trustworthy and brave.

Working so closely with Saul would have had tremendous benefits for David, who was able to be a "fly on the wall" while Saul ran the nation of Israel. He gained valuable experience for when he would take his own place as king.

Mentors and heroes are an important part of shaping who we become as we grow and mature. They give us advice and direction. They are examples to follow when we face troubles and trials in our lives.

How do you feel when someone is chosen for a position of leadership or a promotion, especially if that person is young?

What does "a man after God's own heart" mean to you? How can you foster more of this attitude in yourself?

What things bring you peace when your mind is troubled?

Why are mentors so important to us? Why do we need people to look up to?

Scenic Route

When has someone disliked you for no apparent reason? How did it make you feel? How did you respond to that person?

What causes you to feel threatened? How do those feelings affect the peace in your life? How can you better manage those feelings?

When have you had to leave a relationship or situation because it was so toxic? Who helped you to determine your course of action?

David was young, good looking, and popular. Saul's daughter Michal was in love with him, and Saul's son Jonathan was David's best, most-trusted friend. Everyone liked David and sang his praises—except King Saul.

Read 1 Samuel 18:28-29.

But when Saul realized that the LORD was with David, and that Saul's daughter Michal loved him, 29 Saul was still more afraid of David. So Saul was David's enemy from that time forward.

David was Saul's best and most successful commander. He won far more victories on behalf of Saul than any of Saul's other commanders. One would think that Saul would have been delighted to have David among the ranks of his army. So why was Saul scared of him? Why did he seek to be David's enemy?

The green-eyed monster of jealousy bit Saul when he realized that David was the more popular. Saul sensed that God was with David, as God had once been with him, which angered him and caused him to feel threatened. Feeling threatened and being afraid have many similarities. A normal human reaction is to try to eliminate the threat or the source of the fear.

Saul intentionally put David in harm's way, hoping he would be killed in battle. When those efforts failed, Saul had to become more aggressive. In his mind, all of his troubles could be traced to David, which cemented David as his enemy.

We have all encountered people who, for no apparent reason, dislike us. We've probably also had the same experience in reverse. David didn't know why Saul had come to hate him, but after several attempts on his life, David had good reason to be afraid.

The best way to escape harm is to avoid the source of danger. When David realized the extent of Saul's hatred for him, he fled. Saul's own family aided in David's escape. Saul spent most of the remainder of his life chasing David.

Workers Ahead

Read 1 Samuel 24:1-5.

When Saul returned from following the Philistines, he was told, "David is in the wilderness of En-gedi." 2 Then Saul took three thousand chosen men out of all Israel, and went to look for David and his men in the direction of the Rocks of the Wild Goats. ³ He came to the sheepfolds beside the road, where there was a cave; and Saul went in to relieve himself. Now David and his men were sitting in the innermost parts of the cave. ⁴ The men of David said to him, "Here is the day of which the LORD said to you, 'I will give your enemy into your hand, and you shall do to him as it seems good to you.'" Then David went and stealthily cut off a corner of Saul's cloak. ⁵ Afterward David was stricken to the heart because he had cut off a corner of Saul's cloak.

David eventually hid from Saul in the wilderness, where others joined him. While looking for David, Saul unknowingly stumbled into a cave where David and his men were hiding. David's men tried to convince him that this was the time to take action. Obviously, it would have been a great opportunity to get rid of Saul. They even told him that God had delivered Saul to him, but David refused to harm Saul. Despite the fact that Saul was hunting him and would have killed him given the opportunity, David respected Saul, who was God's anointed.

Many conflicts have arisen over what people felt was a lack of respect for their feelings, opinions, ideals, faith, etc. Our basic understanding of respect is a sense of the worth of a person or deference to a position. David knew that even though Saul had not acted honorably, he was still the king. God had chosen him to lead the Israelites.

Read 1 Samuel 24:8-22.

Afterwards David also rose up and went out of the cave and called after Saul, "My lord the king!" When Saul looked behind him, David bowed with his face to the ground, and did obeisance. ⁹ David said to Saul, "Why do you listen to the words of those who say, 'David seeks to do you harm'? ¹⁰ This very day your eyes have seen how the LORD gave you into my hand in the cave; and some urged me to kill you, but I spared you. I said, 'I will not raise my hand against my lord; for he is the LORD's anointed.' ¹¹ See, my father, see the corner of your cloak in my hand; for by the fact that I cut off the corner of your cloak, and did not kill you, you may know for certain that there is no wrong or treason in my hands. I have not sinned against you, though you are hunting me to take my life. ¹² May the LORD judge between me and you! May the LORD avenge me on you; but my hand shall not be against you. ¹³ As the ancient proverb says, 'Out of the wicked comes forth wickedness'; but my hand shall not be against you. ¹⁴ Against whom has the king of Israel come out? Whom do you pursue? A dead dog? A single flea? ¹⁵ May the LORD therefore be judge, and give sentence between me and you. May he see to it, and plead my cause, and vindicate me against you."

¹⁶ When David had finished speaking these words to Saul, Saul said, "Is this your voice, my son David?" Saul lifted up his voice and wept. ¹⁷ He said to David, "You are more righteous than I; for you have repaid me good, whereas I have repaid you evil. ¹⁸ Today you have explained how you have dealt well with me, in that you did not kill me when the LORD put me into your hands. ¹⁹ For who has ever found an enemy, and sent the enemy safely away? So may the LORD reward you with good for

When have you taken revenge against someone who dislikes you? How did you feel afterward?

To whom do you show respect? Why? What standard do you use to decide whether or not to respect someone? What would cause you not to show respect to someone?

what you have done to me this day. [20] *Now I know that you shall surely be king, and that the kingdom of Israel shall be established in your hand.* [21] *Swear to me therefore by the LORD that you will not cut off my descendants after me, and that you will not wipe out my name from my father's house."* [22] *So David swore this to Saul. Then Saul went home; but David and his men went up to the stronghold.*

Instead of taking the opportunity to kill Saul, David let him leave the cave. Once Saul was a safe distance away, David called to him. With the corner of Saul's cloak as proof, David explained that he could have killed Saul, but chose not to exact revenge. He assured Saul that he wanted peace, not rebellion. Saul heard David's words and saw his actions. He recognized the truth of David's words.

Because David respected Saul and acted honorably toward him, war was averted. Peace prevailed because David respected and trusted the Lord. In a world that is in turmoil with many areas ravaged by war, we should all seek peace. That peace is available only through God.

In the Rear View

In just a short time, David experienced a lot of changes in his young life. Yet even with his youth and inexperience, he trusted God to help him make wise choices. Those choices put him in good standing with the people of Israel, which made it easier for him to assume the role of king after Saul's death.

David did not hesitate to do battle when it was necessary, but he also sought peace. We can seek and work for peace as well. In what areas of your life do you need to work for peace?

What is your role in establishing or maintaining peace? the role of your faith community? In what areas of your life can you promote peace where someone is trying to stir up trouble?

What choices do you trust God to help you make? Do you trust God with the everyday choices or only with the "big" decisions?

Travel Log

Day 1:

God calls each of us to a specific ministry. Write a few words about God's call in your life. How are you fulfilling God's call? Make notes about some other things God might be calling you to do.

Day 2:

We are often quick to criticize our leaders, but seldom do we consider how we can help them. Jot down some current concerns. Pray for your local, state, and national leaders as they deal with those concerns.

Day 3:

Do you have a spiritual mentor? If so, send that person a note to explain what he or she means to you. As you consider this person, use the space below to list some of the things you want to include in your note.

If you do not have a spiritual mentor, think about someone who might be able to fulfill that role for you.

Day 4:

David's men advised him to kill Saul. Think of a time when you were given advice that turned out to be faulty. Write a few sentences about why the advice wasn't good in that situation. What did you learn from the experience?

Day 5:

David knew that he should not harm Saul, even though in the eyes of others he had every right to do so. When have you gone against your conscience or the Holy Spirit in order to achieve a particular goal? What happened? Journal your thoughts.

Day 6:

Even though Saul tried on several occasions to kill him, David still had enough respect for Saul not to take advantage of Saul when he was vulnerable. Think of someone whom you respect and write down why you respect him or her.

Day 7:

List some situations that need peace. Create a separate list of ways you can work for peace in those situations.

Give Peace a Chance

Scripture for lesson:
Isaiah 2:3-5; 11:6-9

Two of the most iconic photos from the Vietnam protests occurred on the same day at nearly the same time. Photographer Bernie Boston took the photo titled "Flower Power." In his photo we see two sides in stark contrast to one another. On one side is a wall of military police, with rifles pointed toward a mass of protesters, ready to protect the Pentagon if violence or disorder should occur. Right in the middle is a young protester who has broken away from the others and is calmly walking down the line of guns, placing a carnation in the end of each barrel. It was such a powerful representation of the anti-war movement that it was nominated for the Pulitzer Prize in 1967, at the height of the Vietnam War.

The other photo, taken by Marc Riboud, is of a 17-year-old high school student, standing in front of a line of military bayonets, holding a daisy forward to an unseen soldier. Both photos show an image of peace and youthful optimism in the face of violence and aggression. One of the things that strikes me the most about both of these pictures is how, by one simple act, these two people each took instruments of death and destruction and turned them into symbols of peace and hope.

Prep for the Journey

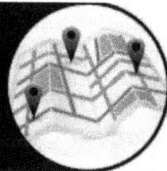

Isaiah was one of the greatest prophets in the Old Testament. His superb writings reflected his education and his knowledge of the religious and political scene—past and present. He came to be incredibly well respected, but during his lifetime that was not the case. He did, however, have a group of disciples who preserved his writings until history proved them to be true.

Isaiah served as prophet during the reign of five different kings. Given his apparent close relationship with these monarchs, as well as his level of education, Isaiah evidently had a significant position

When have you seen something that was meant for destructive purposes used for peace?

in society. His peers in society would have been loath to accept his prophecies; no one likes to be criticized, even when it is deserved and comes as a warning.

The political situation in the area was unstable. Assyria, Egypt, and Babylon were all vying for power, invading and taking captive the peoples of the smaller nations, such as Judah and Israel, as they amassed their empires. Isaiah was resolute in his conviction that Judah and Israel should remain as neutral as possible in these conflicts. In fact, Isaiah was able to influence King Hezekiah to remain neutral, thus delaying the fall of Jerusalem.

As is true with most prophets, Isaiah included, they are ahead of their time. God had given Isaiah a vision of what was in store for Israel and Judah, but few people believed his prophecies. Thankfully, even though few people listened to him, he continued to speak the truth as God revealed it to him.

On the Road

God gave Isaiah glimpses of Israel's future through visions. The things Isaiah saw in those visions weren't always good. As a matter of fact, a large part of the Book of Isaiah talks about the judgment Israel and Judah will face as a result of their disobedience toward God. Such pronouncements can make Isaiah's writings seem very bleak and without hope, but that is far from the truth. He was simply trying to impress upon his people the urgency of the situation; he wanted them to avoid some of the suffering he foresaw.

Read Isaiah 2:3-5.
Many peoples shall come and say,
"Come, let us go up to the mountain of the LORD,
*   to the house of the God of Jacob;*
that he may teach us his ways
*   and that we may walk in his paths."*
For out of Zion shall go forth instruction,
*   and the word of the LORD from Jerusalem.*
⁴ He shall judge between the nations,
*   and shall arbitrate for many peoples;*
they shall beat their swords into plowshares,
*   and their spears into pruning hooks;*
nation shall not lift up sword against nation,
*   neither shall they learn war any more.*
⁵ O house of Jacob,
*   come, let us walk*
*   in the light of the LORD!*

When have you received advice that you later wished you'd followed? What prevented you from seeing the wisdom of that advice earlier?

How is God giving us glimpses of our future? How well do we receive these "prophecies"? What can we learn from these ancient prophecies?

As we read these words, we may think, "Yeah, right. Like that's going to happen." And we would have centuries of history that give credence to our thinking. But Isaiah saw what was possible and wanted to share it with God's people. In the midst of a difficult time for them as a nation, Isaiah's words offered hope for a better future.

Absolute peace will only happen when every nation puts down its weapons, stops fighting, and follows God. We're not talking about a cease fire, or the lull between one war and the beginning of another. Peace will come when we, as human beings, "get it"—when we all finally understand what God has been calling us to be since our creation.

God calls us to be peacemakers, which means putting others first. We must put aside our wishes, our egos, and our desires so that we can help all people. Whether we realize it or not, we are in fellowship with all of creation. When we can begin to see every person we encounter as being part of that fellowship, we will finally see one another as God sees us. Only then will peace truly exist.

Scenic Route

Given the unrest of Isaiah's time, many people may never have experienced a time when they were not in imminent danger of being overtaken, or when they were not at war with someone. Peace was not a part of life for them. They didn't know what it would mean to have peace.

So why would God give Isaiah a vision of peace? Without hope, people despair and don't see a reason to work for a better future. God wanted the people to know that such an existence was possible.

When we look back, we can see with 20/20 vision. Everything Isaiah prophesied has come true through Jesus Christ. But hundreds of years before the birth of Christ, Isaiah brought prophecies of salvation to people who were weary and beaten down by the stresses of their lives.

Isaiah said that God would send a messiah to save the people. This messiah would be a descendant of King David! It's easy for us to look back on the many stories of David and assume that his descendants had great prestige among God's people, but they did not. His royal line was almost completely lost. How in the world could the savior of God's people, the great promised king, come from the family of David? Just look at the social status of Mary and Joseph; they had to stay in a livestock barn! But from those humble beginnings, Jesus came and did everything Isaiah proclaimed.

For centuries, people and nations have tried to establish peace forcibly. What method would you use to establish peace? How can you and your faith community model ways of establishing peace?

Recall a time when you were put in the role of peacemaker. How effective were your efforts? How did your words and actions indicate that you considered all parties to be children of God?

How would you describe peace to someone who has never experienced it? In what areas of our world have some people never experienced peace? How can they work for something they've never known?

What causes you to feel weary and beaten down? How does your knowledge and understanding of Christ as Messiah give you strength to face the future?

Workers Ahead

CAUTION

Read Isaiah 11:6-9.

The wolf shall live with the lamb,
the leopard shall lie down with the kid,
the calf and the lion and the fatling together,
and a little child shall lead them.
⁷ The cow and the bear shall graze,
their young shall lie down together;
and the lion shall eat straw like the ox.
⁸ The nursing child shall play over the hole of the asp,
and the weaned child shall put its hand on the adder's den.
⁹ They will not hurt or destroy
on all my holy mountain;
for the earth will be full of the knowledge of the LORD
as the waters cover the sea.

These scriptures describe the peace that would come about as a result of this descendant of David. He would create a peace, the likes of which the people had not known. The examples he used were ones with which the people would have been familiar: "The wolf will lie down with the lamb"; "the calf and the lion and the yearling will be together"; and "The child will play near to the snake's nest" and will not get hurt. These things were unimaginable at the time. Wolves killed sheep. Lions devoured calves and yearlings. Snakes bit people. It would be like saying that Republicans and Democrats could agree on who should be the president!

I'm not sure we fully understand what it means to have peace in our lives. We get so worked up about buying a certain car, worry that our house isn't nice enough, or become concerned because our child isn't on the honor roll. We allow such worldly things to steal our peace. Yet, to some degree, aren't these things a normal part of living?

How do we take ourselves out of that cycle, that rat race? How can we change the way we live and interact with our world? We have to make a conscious effort to choose to live differently. We have to choose to live for more than our favorite sports team. We have to choose to live for more than our job. God has called us to live and work for a purpose bigger than what we see in this physical world. We have to choose to live out God's calling on our life.

How can we create peace in our lives during times of turmoil? What role does/could your faith community have in creating that peace?

What could you put aside that would help you to have more peace in your life? What is keeping you from doing so?

What do you think would happen if we all lived out God's calling on our lives? How might that contribute to peace?

In the Rear View

Isaiah was one of the greatest prophets in the history of the Israelite people. He glimpsed the peace that would be possible for Israel. He saw what God's chosen people could become. He also saw the difficulties they would face because they had turned away from God. Isaiah prophesied that peace was coming; however, he didn't say when, where, or how. When peace came in the form of the Messiah, most of the people didn't recognize it because he didn't come as they had expected.

It is difficult for us to recognize peace in our own lives because we've become so accustomed to the chaos we see and feel every day. We don't achieve peace by continuing to do the same things we've always done. We have to decide to live differently. We have to turn away from the status quo. We have to turn toward God.

How will you seek God's peace? How can you help others to find peace?

Travel Log

Day 1:

The two images mentioned in the opening story were iconic images of peace during a time of war. Draw a picture or write a story of what peace looks like in our world today.

Day 2:

Think about some of the advice that people gave you when you were younger. Did you follow that advice? Describe what that advice was and what you would do differently if it had been given today.

Day 3:

Isaiah desperately wanted the Israelites to avoid the suffering that he foresaw. Describe a moment when you tried to help someone avoid a difficult situation. Were your efforts successful? What did you learn?

Day 4:

As human beings, we always struggle with how we view ourselves and one another. God sees us as we truly are. Write down how you think God wants us to see one another.

Day 5:

    Think of a time when you felt that you were in a terrible situation or had made a bad decision. As you look back on that time, what good came from it? Explain why you can now see it as a positive experience.

Day 6:

    The world tells us that certain things are essential for us to be happy and at peace. Often the struggle to get these material items cause us more stress than if we just learned to be happy with what we already have. Identify something you really think would make your life happier and less stressful. Write down three reasons you believe it would make you happy, and three reasons it might make your life worse.

Day 7:

Allowing stress to overwhelm us can weaken our faith. We can't continue to live in the same way and expect our lives to change. Write down three different ways that you can live a more peaceful, God-centered life.

Lending a Helping Hand

Scripture for lesson:
Luke 10:25-37

L FAITH LIFE F E

When has someone you didn't know helped you in a difficult situation? When have you been able to help someone who was experiencing difficult circumstances?

On December 24, 2013, I was traveling from Quitman, Louisiana, to Monticello, Arkansas, where I would officiate at the annual Christmas Eve communion service for my home church, Rose Hill Cumberland Presbyterian. Less than half a mile from the Arkansas-Louisiana border, I fell asleep at the wheel. My little car ran off the road and hit a tree, flipping three times in the process. At the moment my car started to flip, the mother of my sister's best friend was coming down the other side of the highway. Even though she didn't know I was the person involved in the accident, she stopped to help. Since she is a nurse, she made me lie down and began to check me for serious injuries.

This woman was a tremendous comfort to me in that situation. Her presence calmed me while she checked for injuries. It was a blessing that my injuries were nothing more than a pulled muscle in my back, a bruise on my chest, and a very gnarly scrape on my right shin. I was blessed that someone immediately stopped to help me at one of the most stressful, scary times of my life. As I reflect on what happened, I don't know what I would have done if I had been in her shoes.

Prep for the Journey

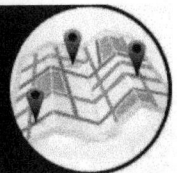

People, especially the Jewish religious leaders or their pawns, frequently questioned Jesus. They were hoping to trick him into saying something that was not in agreement with the Law of Moses, to which they strictly adhered. If Jesus said something against the Law, the leaders could discredit him with the people and put an end to this movement that was becoming such a threat to their way of life.

How do you react to things that threaten your way of life? Why?

Read Luke 10:25-28.

Just then a lawyer stood up to test Jesus. "Teacher," he said, "what must I do to inherit eternal life?" 26 He said to him, "What is written in the law? What do you read there?" 27 He answered, "You shall love the Lord your God with all your heart, and with all your soul, and with all your strength, and with all your mind; and your neighbor as yourself." 28 And he said to him, "You have given the right answer; do this, and you will live."

In Jesus' time, lawyers were extremely well-versed in the Mosaic Law and were regarded as authorities in its interpretation. Knowing this, Jesus tossed the ball back to the lawyer by saying, "You know the law. What does it say?"

Of course the lawyer knew the answer. "It tells us to love the Lord, our God, and to love our neighbors as ourselves."

Can't you almost hear Jesus say, maybe even with some exasperation, "Well, if you know what you're supposed to do, then go and do it"? What Jesus didn't say at this time was that no one could be saved by following the Law.

The original Laws of Moses had been given by God and included the Ten Commandments. However, over the years, humans had added to the Law until it became so unwieldy that no one could keep it perfectly. Even if keeping the Law had been able to save people, observing every detail of it was impossible.

On the Road

Measuring himself against both of these commands, the lawyer undoubtedly thought he was doing pretty well in regards to loving God, but he wasn't sure about loving his neighbors. So he asked Jesus who his neighbor was. The lawyer surely knew the intent behind the laws, but he may have been looking for a loophole. He wanted to know how he could follow the letter of the law, instead of the spirit of the law. But he wasn't prepared to hear what it meant to love one's neighbors.

Read Luke 10:29-33.

But wanting to justify himself, he asked Jesus, "And who is my neighbor?" 30 Jesus replied, "A man was going down from Jerusalem to Jericho, and fell into the hands of robbers, who stripped him, beat him, and went away, leaving him half dead. 31 Now by chance a priest was going down that road; and when he saw him, he passed by on the other side. 32 So likewise a Levite, when he came to the place and saw him, passed by on the other side. 33 But a Samaritan while traveling came near him; and when he saw him, he was moved with pity.

How often do you try to avoid doing what you know you are supposed to do? Why do you try to avoid those actions?

How do you feel about those people who live a law-abiding life, but do not have a relationship with Jesus? How can you help them to understand that living right isn't enough?

When have you or someone you know tried to use "the letter of the law" to justify your actions, even though the real intent was known? Why are people predisposed to try to justify their actions?

How helpful do you find the use of parables? What might be a modern version of this story?

When have you passed by someone who needed help (physically, emotionally)? Thinking back on it now, what would you do differently? Why?

When have you condemned someone's actions without having a full understanding of the situation? How did you feel upon learning more?

Jesus frequently used the storytelling device of a parable to help his listeners understand his message. His parables included every day examples with which the people would have been familiar. In this case he told about a man who was traveling from Jerusalem to Jericho. As he was going down the road, thieves robbed and wounded the traveler, leaving him for dead. He needed help in the worst way possible.

After he was robbed, at least three people passed by this severely wounded man. The first person to pass was a priest. Priests were supposed to be the holiest of all Jewish people. If anyone was going to help this man, if anyone was going to show the compassion of God, it should have been the priest. The priest heard the man moaning and begging for help, so he did the only logical thing and crossed the road, so that he could pretend the man wasn't there.

The next person to come by was a Levite. I like to imagine that he at least walked over to see what had happened to this traveler. Unfortunately, he did almost the same thing as the priest, kind of rubber-necking this incident. He was curious about what had happened, but didn't feel the need to help.

Scenic Route

The journey from Jericho to Jerusalem was almost seventeen miles long and was well known for being dangerous. Given the more than 3,400 foot difference in elevation between the two cities, it would have been a difficult journey, at best. The path would have been narrow and strewn with rocks, requiring travelers to watch their footing very closely. Such conditions made it easy for robbers to take advantage of travelers. The lawyer to whom Jesus was talking, and the others listening to this exchange, would've known this all too well. They would've known the feeling of making the journey, wondering where an attack might come from.

While we are often quick to condemn the priest and the Levite, consider their situation a little more closely. All Jewish people were subject to the laws of cleanliness. Contact with a dead body rendered a person unclean, usually for a certain length of time and until a ritual purification could be performed.

Priests and Levites were not required to live in Jerusalem; therefore, it's quite possible that one or both of them were headed to Jerusalem where they would serve at the Temple. Since there were more priests and Levites than opportunities to serve at the Temple, that might have been their one chance. To be called to serve at the Temple would have been the epitome of their service. However, being ritually unclean would have made them ineligible to serve. While this information in no way excuses their behavior, it can give us some possible insight into their behavior.

Too often, people help those who are in need only as a way to further their own agendas. While their acts may produce some of the desired results (money for a homeless shelter or raising awareness of an issue), they fall short of Jesus' message. When we act only as a way to benefit ourselves, we are not loving our neighbor as ourselves.

Workers Ahead

To Jewish people, Samaritans were lower than dirt. Jewish travelers would take a longer route to keep from going through Samaria. They ignored and treated with contempt those who lived there. The feeling was mutual. Yet the Samaritan was the one who stopped to help.

Read Luke 10:34-35.

He went to him and bandaged his wounds, having poured oil and wine on them. Then he put him on his own animal, brought him to an inn, and took care of him. [35] The next day he took out two denarii, gave them to the innkeeper, and said, "Take care of him; and when I come back, I will repay you whatever more you spend."

Jesus' story continued with a rather shocking turn: A Samaritan stopped to help the wounded traveler. He provided first aid, took him to the nearest inn, and cared for him. Chances are that he delayed his business in order to help the wounded traveler.

When the Samaritan had to leave the next day, he gave the innkeeper money to care for the man. The Samaritan even promised to come back and pay for any extra expenses the innkeeper might incur. The Samaritan didn't just help the man; he made personal sacrifices.

Given the mutual hatred between Jews and Samaritans, Jesus' listeners would likely have expected the Samaritan to finish off the wounded man. Imagine their astonishment when he was the one who stopped to help. This parable is known as the Good Samaritan, but Jews at the time would never have used those words in the same sentence!

Read Luke 10:36-37.

Which of these three, do you think, was a neighbor to the man who fell into the hands of the robbers?" [37] He said, "The one who showed him mercy." Jesus said to him, "Go and do likewise."

The lawyer had thought to put Jesus in a difficult situation with his question, but Jesus turned the tables on him. Jesus' parable suggests that loving our neighbors means seeking out those who are in

Who has helped you when you were in need? How receptive were you to that help? Why?

How do you think the traveler, who is assumed to have been Jewish, felt when he realized that his rescuer was a Samaritan? How do you think the Samaritan felt when he realized that the injured person was Jewish?

How aware are you of people around you who need help? What are you willing to do to help them? What is God calling you and your faith community to do?

To whom would you be unable to offer compassion? Why?

need so that we can offer compassion, despite our prejudices. The lawyer had such a strong disdain for Samaritans that he could not even bring himself to utter the word in response to Jesus' question.

The lesson behind this parable is one of compassion and kindness. Compassion causes us to feel sympathy for people. It makes us want to do more than offer a prayer and continue on our way. It rouses us to volunteer with charities, feed the hungry, and shelter the homeless. Real compassion costs something, whether it is time, effort, or money. But when we show real compassion, we demonstrate our relationship with God and with Jesus Christ.

In the Rear View

In the beginning of this scripture passage, the lawyer was seeking vindication for his own life and actions. But Jesus effectively turned his question, "Who is my neighbor?" so that the lawyer had to ask himself: "What kind of neighbor am I?" We know what the religious folks did when they saw a bruised and battered man left to die on the side of the road. They kept walking. In fact, they crossed to the other side of the road and kept walking.

Ultimately, we have to look at this parable and ask ourselves: Who are we? Are we looking for loopholes that justify our own behavior? When we see someone who needs help, do we pass on by, acting like we have better things to do? Or are we willing to stop and help, to give aid and comfort when we see a person in need, regardless of what it costs us?

Travel Log

Day 1:

We have all seen people in difficult or trying situations. Many of us have helped or been helped by neighbors. Identify someone who needs help and see what you can do to show compassion and care. Then journal about the experience in the space below.

Day 2:

Some of us have been in the place of the traveler by the side of the road. All of us have needed help of one kind or another at some point. Write a note of thanks to a person who has helped you in a time of need. Use the space below to write down some words and ideas you want to include in your note.

Day 3:

The lawyer in this encounter tried to use the letter of the Law to justify his own desires. He wanted to ignore the intent behind the Law. Explain how you have used the Bible to justify your beliefs instead of using the Bible to inform your beliefs.

Day 4:

Given the current culture, people are hesitant to become involved when they see someone in need of assistance. We don't want to risk giving a ride to a stranded motorist; we want to help the homeless man who stands on the street corner, but we don't want to give him money for liquor; we feel for those people who do not have shelter on a cold night, but it's dangerous to take them into our churches or homes.

Write about a situation where someone needs help, but you are afraid to become involved. As you write, consider what methods of offering help are available.

Day 5:

There are so many people who are in need. Find a local food bank, clothes closet, or another ministry that helps those who are less fortunate. Volunteer for an afternoon. Write your reflections about the experience here.

Day 6:

It seems that the more opportunities we have to learn about other people, the more separate we become. The Jewish people hated the Samaritans. How do you feel about offering humanitarian aid to countries that are enemies of the United States? How do you feel about offering compassion to mass murderers? Write a few sentences to express your feelings. Be honest with yourself.

Day 7:

The religious leaders in this parable treated the traveler in need abominably. Write a few suggestions for what you can do so that those outside the church will know that you are a follower of Christ.

Virtue and Vice

Scripture for lesson:
Galatians 5:16-26

I live with two cats that I love as if they were my children. As I watch my friends raise their children, I have come to the conclusion that having cats is somewhat similar to living with toddlers. They wake you up way too early in the morning, and they pester you incessantly until you give them what they want. You constantly have to clean up after them. Both parents and pet owners know that, while silence used to be a welcome break, it is now a cause for concern and investigation. Animals and children can be wild, jealous, greedy, and completely self-centered. But they can be also be loving, kind, and gentle. They will bring you more joy than you can ever imagine.

Prep for the Journey

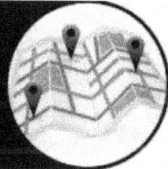

Galatia was a large Roman province whose borders changed frequently. Since Paul did not give any specifics about the churches in this province, we cannot pinpoint the exact locations of these groups of followers. According to Acts, Paul visited this area twice before writing this letter.

The Christians in Galatia would have primarily been converts from pagan religions. Of course, there may also have been some Jewish Christians and other Gentile converts in the group. By this time, the original group of followers had spread throughout much of the Roman Empire as a result of persecution.

Paul came under fire from a group of Jewish Christians who were called Judaizers. Because Paul had not been one of the original apostles, these believers accused him of not preaching the truth. As Jewish converts, they believed the church of Galatia had to follow all of the Laws of Moses, including being circumcised, in order to receive salvation. Paul, having once been a Pharisee, understood the conflict in their beliefs, but he had also experienced the saving grace of Christ.

What brings you joy? How do you share your joy?

When have your beliefs put you at odds with other believers? How were you able to achieve peace in spite of your differences?

When have you substituted good actions or being a good person for a true relationship with Christ? What caused you to realize the difference?

What might cause a mass exodus of believers in today's church? How would such an exodus relate to the truth of what's being taught?

Paul was raised in a Jewish home, taught to follow the Mosaic Law, and studied under the best Jewish teacher of that time. He would have taken great pride in how well he followed the Law. It took a personal encounter with the risen Christ to convince Paul that adherence to the Law could not save him. In other words, our actions cannot save us.

The new Gentile Christians did not have the same history with the Law of Moses. They couldn't see why it was necessary to become Jewish in order to believe in Christ; Paul agreed. However, the Judaizers sought to discredit Paul and nearly caused a mass exodus of believers from the churches in Galatia.

On the Road

Paul began the fifth chapter of his letter to the Galatians by saying that Christ has set us free from sin. He then warned the Galatian Christians of the dangers of falling back into their old habits and ways of living. Paul knew the dangers of them turning away from the gospel, and was very disturbed about the false teachers among them.

Read Galatians 5:16-18.

Live by the Spirit, I say, and do not gratify the desires of the flesh. [17]For what the flesh desires is opposed to the Spirit, and what the Spirit desires is opposed to the flesh; for these are opposed to each other, to prevent you from doing what you want. [18] But if you are led by the Spirit, you are not subject to the law.

All persons have two different forces inside of them that pull in opposite directions. The sinful nature pulls persons toward self-gratification and lawlessness, which keeps them tethered to the physical world. Opposing the sinful nature is the Holy Spirit, which pulls believers toward what God desires for them. When people live by the Spirit, they do not want to follow their sinful nature.

When have you let your sinful nature control your decision-making, even though you knew it was the wrong choice? What was the outcome?

Christ freed people from the shackles of living by the Law. We are free to live by the new commands: to love God, to live unselfishly, to think of others, to help those in distress, to be kind and generous even to people whom we might not like. I am free to live my life without holding grudges or trying to measure my worth against someone else. Our eternity is not determined by how closely we follow the rules, but by how much we let our teacher, Jesus, change our lives.

How does making a commitment to live by new commands free us? In what other areas of your life have you found this to be true?

It is very easy to become tangled up in saying that "real Christians" follow the rules this way, or "real faith" is lived out like this. However, when we start trying to live by these arbitrary rules, strict standards, and special conditions, we once again become slaves to laws that are impossible to live by. Christ wants us to live free of the worry that comes with falling short of perfection.

Scenic Route

The Holy Spirit is infinitely stronger than our sinful nature. The problem is that we often go out of our way to do the thing we know is worst for us. We rely on ourselves, on our own experiences, and our own wisdom to make decisions. That is why we fail so often and relapse into our old ways of living. There is only one way that we can overcome our sinful nature, and that is by trusting in the Holy Spirit to guide us.

Read Galatians 5:19-21.

Now the works of the flesh are obvious: fornication, impurity, licentiousness, [20] idolatry, sorcery, enmities, strife, jealousy, anger, quarrels, dissensions, factions, [21] envy, drunkenness, carousing, and things like these. I am warning you, as I warned you before: those who do such things will not inherit the kingdom of God.

Paul listed several examples of vices to which our sinful nature is drawn. Many of the behaviors are things that we would instantly identify as destructive or evil, such as immorality, sorcery, drunkenness, and enmity. Some of the behaviors, like envy, jealousy, and impurity, we might rank as being not quite as bad for us as the first few.

But let's get a little different perspective on these verses by reading them from The Message Bible:

It is obvious what kind of life develops out of trying to get your own way all the time: repetitive, loveless, cheap sex; a stinking accumulation of mental and emotional garbage; frenzied and joyless grabs for happiness; trinket gods; magic-show religion; paranoid loneliness; cutthroat competition; all-consuming-yet-never-satisfied wants; a brutal temper; an impotence to love or be loved; divided homes and divided lives; small-minded and lopsided pursuits; the vicious habit of depersonalizing everyone into a rival; uncontrolled and uncontrollable addictions; ugly parodies of community. I could go on.

This isn't the first time I have warned you, you know. If you use your freedom this way, you will not inherit God's kingdom.

This interpretation puts the scripture into words that are more relevant and understandable for us. Unfortunately, many of the things described are thought to be necessary to achieve success, or at least accompany success.

In Paul's time, Christians were dealing with all of these things. The people to whom Paul was speaking were interacting daily with people who were worshiping idols, participating in religious orgies, becoming drunk, and engaging in debauchery. Since many of the Galatian Christians had come from this background, it was natural for them to fall back into what was familiar.

When things such as drunkenness, sex outside of marriage, and partying are so widely accepted in our culture, how can we effectively represent the Bible's teachings without alienating people from the gospel?

How closely do you think this interpretation of the scripture reflects the world in which we live? Why?

How do you characterize success? How can the church help people to realize that success is not dependent upon these things listed in the passage of scripture?

Workers Ahead

Paul gave the Galatians a list of negatives, but he followed it with a list of positives. According to Paul, Christians should be filled with and exhibit these things.

Read Galatians 5:22-26.

By contrast, the fruit of the Spirit is love, joy, peace, patience, kindness, generosity, faithfulness, ²³ gentleness, and self-control. There is no law against such things. ²⁴ And those who belong to Christ Jesus have crucified the flesh with its passions and desires. ²⁵ If we live by the Spirit, let us also be guided by the Spirit. ²⁶ Let us not become conceited, competing against one another, envying one another.

It's funny that these are called fruits of the Spirit. When they hear the word fruit, people tend to think of oranges, apples, and grapes, but these fruits are traits that grow in us when we strive to live a Christ-filled life. Love, joy, peace, patience, kindness, goodness, faithfulness, gentleness, and self-control are the byproduct of letting the Spirit be in control of our lives. We must follow, love, imitate, and know the Spirit. When we do so, we fulfill the command to love God and love our neighbors as ourselves.

Each of these spiritual gifts is part of the other. We need all of the other fruits if we want peace. If we don't have self-control then we are unlikely to be patient. Love and peace create kindness. They are all intertwined. If we have one, we have the others; if we are missing one, we are missing the others.

God is interested in every aspect of our lives. If we want to live by the Spirit then we've got to submit all parts of our lives: spiritual, emotional, physical, social, and even our work lives to God's control. Only by submitting to God's control will we know peace.

In the Rear View

If our greatest desire is to achieve the fruits of the Spirit, then we know that the Spirit is truly guiding our lives. We must live each day with the Holy Spirit as our guide. When we work to live according to God's will for us, the words of Christ will be in our hearts, the love of Christ will be behind our actions, and the power of Christ will sustain us.

Will we sometimes slip and give in to our sinful natures? Yes! But when we do, God's love and grace is available to us.

How do the fruits of the spirit contribute to peace?

What does it mean to submit all parts of our lives to God's control? Why is this submission necessary for peace?

Travel Log

Day 1:

List three ways that you have been set free from sin. How has this freedom changed the way you live?

Day 2:

Describe some moments when you have used your beliefs to judge how others live their lives. How can you prevent yourself from judging others in the future?

Day 3:

We constantly have two forces pulling us in different directions: our sinful nature and the Holy Spirit. Journal about a time when you experienced this struggle and what happened.

Day 4:

Many of the vices that Paul listed appeal to our sinful nature. List the three vices you struggle with the most. Then list the three vices that you feel are most harmful to the world.

Day 5:

Look again at the vices Paul named. Write down the ones you believe to be the least harmful. Compare this list to the one you created for Day 4. Why do you think some of them are worse than others? How has modern society influenced your thinking?

Day 6:

The fruits of the Spirit can be difficult for us to attain. Which of these traits do you think is easiest to attain? Which is the hardest for you to achieve? Describe why.

Day 7:
Write down each of the spiritual gifts. Beside each gift, list someone you know who embodies that gift.

Peace Sayings of Christ

Scripture for lesson:
Matthew 5:9; Luke 19:42;
John 14:27; 16:33

LIFE FAITH

If you want to see the measure of a person, pay attention to how he or she treats subordinates. For the last few months, I have been working part-time as a cashier at a large retail chain/grocery store. Most of the customers who have come through my checkout line have been a joy to serve. They are nice. They are interesting. Thankfully, most of my customers have been very understanding when I have made major mistakes. However, three or four people were so unhappy that nothing would have made them happy. I've had people curse me, scream at me, and call me every name in the book.

When someone lashes out at me, it can be difficult to hold my tongue. When I was younger, I had a terrible temper. As I matured, I learned to keep my temper in check. I hope that people who know me now see me as a kind, funny guy who tries to avoid conflict. When conflict does arise, I try to be objective and look for the fairest solution possible and maintain peace.

Prep for the Journey

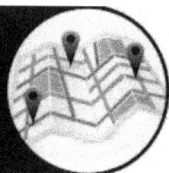

The Sermon on the Mount, which begins with the Beatitudes, was given at the beginning of Jesus' public ministry. Some people think the teachings given in this sermon are too numerous to have been given at one time. It's possible that Matthew collected them and put them into a single discourse. Regardless of when they were given, these teachings formed the basis for a completely new way of life. For those who followed Jesus, they replaced the Torah, or books of Law, as a guide for living.

Read Matthew 5:9.
"Blessed are the peacemakers, for they will be called children of God."
The Beatitudes are promises of God's kingdom and descriptions of those who will receive the promises. Although these people are not

What does your reaction to another's anger say about you? How can you remain calm and peaceful in the face of others' anger?

How would the world be different if we truly used the Beatitudes as a guide for living?

Think of a time when you have been a peacemaker or have benefited from the efforts of one. How did you feel? How were the peacemaker's efforts received?

When have you been a thermometer person? Share about that experience. Do you consider yourself to be more of a thermostat or a thermometer person? Why?

When have you experienced a thermostat person's influence? What alerted you to this person's ability to affect the climate positively?

When have you been able to trust without doubts or misgivings? What enabled you to trust to this degree? How did it bring you peace?

perfect, they are seeking God's kingdom. Those who love and pursue peace will be known as God's children.

It can be helpful to look at the Beatitudes as a flight of stairs, with each statement moving closer to real joy. The Beatitude above is the seventh out of eight Beatitudes Matthew lists. It might be so high on the list because it takes a lot of maturity to be a peacemaker.

Someone once said that there are two kinds of people: "thermostat" people and "thermometer" people. A thermometer reflects the climate of the room, but a thermostat can change the climate. A thermostat person can change the climate of the room just by entering it. Some thermostat people cause conflict, almost as if it is part of their DNA. However, peacemakers are also thermostat people, and they have a positive influence over the climate.

Most people have experienced situations in which it seemed that everyone was complaining and everything was going wrong. Then a thermostat person walked into the room, and the whole climate changed. God wants us to strive to be peacemakers in the church and in the world. Such people concentrate on the positive and see the good things God is doing in the church and in the world.

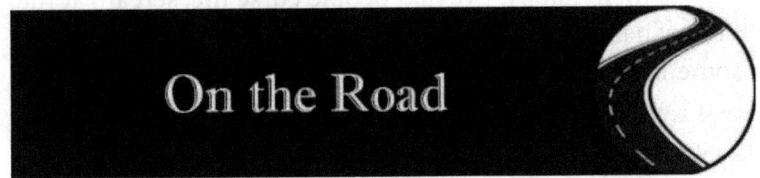

On the Road

We tend to think of peace as an absence of conflict. While that is one meaning of peace, there are others. When we have a right relationship with God, we will know peace even if turmoil surrounds us. Such peace can come only from God.

Read John 14:27.

"Peace I leave with you; my peace I give to you. I do not give to you as the world gives. Do not let your hearts be troubled, and do not let them be afraid."

Jesus uttered these words very near the end of his ministry. Jesus knew that he would soon be facing his own death, yet he gave peace to his disciples. By offering them his peace, Jesus was giving them what they would need to get through the times ahead: the ability to trust wholeheartedly in God. When they were able to accept Christ's gift, there would be no doubts or misgivings because they would be at peace.

Sin, fear, and uncertainty are at war in each of us. When we try to find peace through our own efforts or through worldly things, we fail dismally. The only way to find deep and lasting peace is by seeking Christ and allowing the Holy Spirit to guide us.

When we have Christ in our lives, we will still experience times of conflict. But peace in Christ means that we no longer have to worry about the present or the future. We can take comfort in knowing that the stress we are currently facing is only temporary, but our life with Christ is eternal.

Scenic Route

During Jesus' time, a common greeting was "God be with you." It was a prayer of sorts. Many churches have a point during the worship service where they "pass the peace." The usual form of the greeting is, "May the peace of Christ be with you." The response is, "And also with you." I wonder how many times we utter these words without thinking about what we are saying.

Read John 16:33.

"I have said this to you, so that in me you may have peace. In the world you face persecution. But take courage; I have conquered the world!"

In the verse just prior to the one above, Jesus told the disciples that they would scatter and leave him alone. He knew that he would soon be arrested and that the disciples would dessert him, yet he still wanted them to have peace.

Maybe Jesus was thinking of the guilt, shame, and humiliation the disciples would experience as a result of their desertion. He did not want them to become so focused on their failures that they could not continue with the work he had started. By telling them that they had peace through him, Jesus was forgiving them in advance for their worldly failures, which he had already conquered.

It is an amazing feeling to come to a church, to be part of a denomination, to go to conferences and retreats, where everyone loves and respects you. It's exciting when you are around people with whom you agree. It's great to be around people who know you and appreciate you for simply being yourself. However, we were never promised lives free from the worries of the world. It was never promised that we would get along with everyone. We were never promised an easy life. We were promised a life where we would never have to face our troubles by ourselves. Jesus will never abandon us, even in our most trying circumstances. Our victory has already been won, and we get to claim the prize Christ won on our behalf more than 2000 years ago.

What does the peace of Christ mean to you? What do you think most people associate with the "peace of Christ"? How can we share that peace in the midst of conflict and suffering?

When have you felt like you disappointed Christ? How were you able to find peace in that situation? What level of courage was required to overcome the situation?

What is the difference in finding peace in a known situation as opposed to an unknown one? What helps you to find peace in unknown circumstances?

Workers Ahead

How can you find peace in work situations? in situations over which you have no control?

For sixteen years I worked at a dry cleaners and laundry that my family owned. It was a wonderful experience to hang out with my grandmother and wait on customers. I was generally happy to go to work each day. After my grandmother sold the cleaners and I began working for someone who wasn't related to me, I experienced a dose of reality. I found out that working for someone else would never be all sunshine and roses.

Read Luke 19:42.

"If you, even you, had only recognized on this day the things that make for peace! But now they are hidden from your eyes."

Jesus had just experienced one of the human highlights of his ministry. It had to have been gratifying to hear crowds of people praising him. Many of those present had recognized Jesus as the promised messiah and were ready for him to take the throne as king. Of course, we now know that Jesus was not the type of messiah they expected.

What types of situations cause you to want to cry? Why? How are those situations like the one Jesus faced as he prepared to enter Jerusalem?

Jesus' emotions were bound to have been like a roller coaster that day. He knew what was coming—for himself, his followers, and for those who had opposed him. Before descending into Jerusalem, Jesus stopped and looked over the city. Then Jesus did something recorded only once before in all the New Testament: He wept.

The word *Jerusalem* is believed to have meant "vision of peace." As Jesus looked at this city, the center of worship for God's people, he did not see peace. Instead Jesus saw the future of Israel. He saw the possibilities of what could have been if the people had listened to and understood his teachings. He knew that his followers would face tragedy and persecution. It's no wonder Jesus cried.

Jesus had come to bring peace, but many of the people continued to reject him. They chose instead the empty offerings of the world, which caused them to become even more destitute spiritually. For centuries God's messengers had been telling the people how to live in accordance with God's will. At times the people would turn from their worldly ways and follow God, but eventually they would return to lives separate from God. Finally God sent his own son to communicate this message, but they rejected him as well. Because of their rejection, they could not see the way to peace.

How do you think the world today compares to the situation in Jesus' time? Why? What are you doing to help people find the peace of Christ?

50

In the Rear View

Jesus Christ is known by many names, including Good Shepherd, the Great Physician, and the Word. The one that possibly best describes his ministry is Prince of Peace. Christ came to bring peace to the entire world and to every part of our lives. Too often we try to create our own peace and happiness, but it is a futile effort. The only way to true, lasting peace is found by answering God's call on our lives and accepting Christ as our savior.

Which name for Christ is the most meaningful to you? Why?

Travel Log

Day 1:

Read the Beatitudes as found in Matthew 5:3-11. Write another one to add to the list. Where would you place it?

Day 2:

Think of a time when a conflict arose between two people. What did you do to diffuse the situation? Write down your response to two friends who might be upset with each other.

Day 3:

We are called to be peacemakers in all aspects of our lives. Identify ways you can be a peacemaker in your home, at work, with your friends, and at church.

Day 4:

List some actions you can take to achieve peace in your personal life in the midst of turmoil. Note some specific places where you will implement those actions.

Day 5:

Jesus told his disciples that he had conquered the world. What evidence do you see that Jesus has indeed conquered the world? Write a few words of praise or compose a prayer that reflects your thoughts.

Day 6:

The world around Jesus was in turmoil. Write a few words or sentences about a time when your life was in turmoil. How did Christ give you the peace and patience to come through that time?

Day 7:

Wars are raging all over the world. Our country has military personnel stationed in places where their lives are daily at risk. Take time now to pray for the safety of those who are in our armed forces. Pray for their families. Pray that all people will seek Christ's peace.

Jot down the names of any men or women you know who are serving in the armed forces. Pray specifically for them. Send them a letter, or even an e-mail, so they know you are praying for them.